Place Value

Written by **Kathy Furgang**

Illustrations by **Jackie Snider**

New York

This book belongs to

_____

New York

An Imprint of Sterling Publishing
387 Park Avenue South
New York, NY 10016

FLASH KIDS, STERLING, and the distinctive Sterling logo are registered trademarks of
Sterling Publishing Co., Inc.

Text and illustrations © 2006 by Flash Kids

Cover design and production by Mada Design, Inc.

ISBN 978-1-4114-3459-2

Distributed in Canada by Sterling Publishing
c/o Canadian Manda Group, 165 Dufferin Street
Toronto, Ontario, Canada M6K 3H6
Distributed in the United Kingdom by GMC Distribution Services
Castle Place, 166 High Street, Lewes, East Sussex, England BN7 1XU
Distributed in Australia by Capricorn Link (Australia) Pty. Ltd.
P.O. Box 704, Windsor, NSW 2756, Australia

For information about custom editions, special sales, and premium and
corporate purchases, please contact Sterling Special Sales
at 800-805-5489 or specialsales@sterlingpublishing.com.

Manufactured in China

Lot #:
4 6 8 10 9 7 5
07/15

www.flashkids.com

Dear Parent,

One of the keys to a lifetime love of math is the development of basic math skills, such as identifying the place value of numbers. Once your child can identify place value, the door will be open to unlimited learning of math. This book teaches place value through fun activities such as matching, filling in the blanks, and coloring. To get the most out of this book, follow these simple steps:

- Find a comfortable place where you and your child can work quietly together.
- Encourage your child to work at his or her own pace.
- Help your child read the words and sentences, and ask questions about the content of what he or she has read.
- Offer lots of praise and support.
- Reward your child's hard work with the included stickers.
- Most of all, remember that learning should be fun! Take time to look at the pictures, laugh at the funny characters, and enjoy this special time spent together.

Let's Party!

Place value tells how large or small a number is.

It tells how many ones, tens, or hundreds are in a number.

hundreds place tens place ones place

There are 2 hundreds.

There are 3 tens.

There are 6 ones.

Wrapped with a Bow

Write how many groups of ten there are.

1. _____

2. _____

3. _____

Bring in the Clowns

Write the number.

1. 4 tens and 3 ones = _____

2. 2 tens and 9 ones = _____

3. 3 tens and 2 ones = _____

4. 1 ten and 1 one = _____

5. 2 tens and 0 ones = _____

6. 1 ten and 4 ones = _____

7. 4 tens and 9 ones = _____

8. 3 tens and 5 ones = _____

9. 6 tens and 0 ones = _____

10. 5 tens and 5 ones = _____

Where Did Everybody Go?

Write the number of tens and ones.

1. 74 = _____ tens and _____ ones

2. 52 = _____ tens and _____ ones

3. 49 = _____ tens and _____ ones

4. 37 = _____ tens and _____ ones

5. 10 = _____ ten and _____ ones

6. 69 = _____ tens and _____ ones

7. 73 = _____ tens and _____ ones

8. 55 = _____ tens and _____ ones

9. 68 = _____ tens and _____ ones

10. 42 = _____ tens and _____ ones

Time for Cake

Circle the number in the tens place.

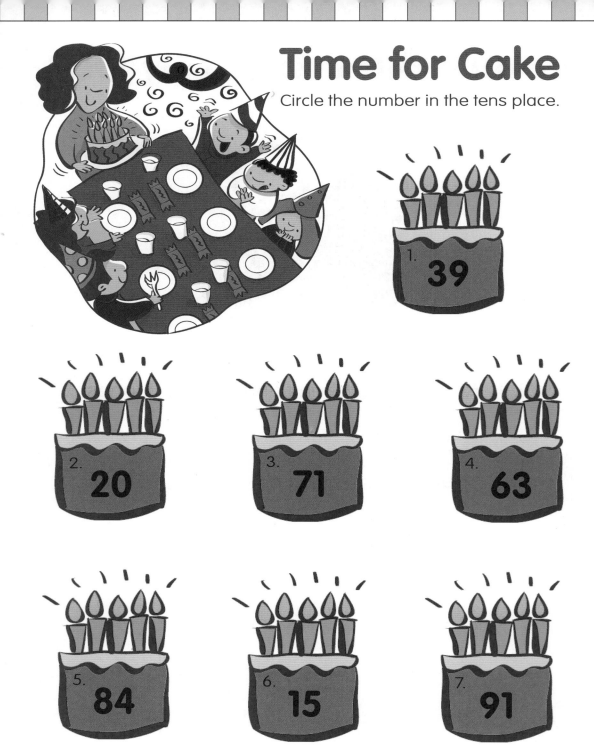

1. 39

2. 20

3. 71

4. 63

5. 84

6. 15

7. 91

Make Some Noise!

Color the noisemakers with **4** in the ones place.

56

45

14

34

49

4

24

So Many Candles

Write how many tens there are. Write how many
ones there are. Write the number on the line.

1.

2 tens and 4 ones = _____

2.

_____ tens and _____ ones = _____

3.

_____ tens and _____ ones = _____

4.

_____ ten and _____ ones = _____

Snack Time

Write the number.

1.   4 tens and 2 ones = _____

2.   9 tens and 1 one = _____

3.   1 ten and 0 ones = _____

4.   0 tens and 5 ones = _____

5.   3 tens and 9 ones = _____

6.   3 tens and 6 ones = _____

7.   7 tens and 2 ones = _____

8.   5 tens and 9 ones = _____

9.   2 tens and 2 ones = _____

10. 4 tens and 6 ones = _____

Everybody Loves a Party

Write the number. Then color the gift that shows the correct answer.

1. 1 hundred + 3 tens + 7 ones =

_____

2. 2 hundreds + 1 ten + 9 ones =

_____

3. 1 hundred + 2 tens + 8 ones =

_____

We Like Cake!

Circle the number in the hundreds place.

1. 821
2. 158
3. 571
4. 369
5. 870
6. 300

Game Time

Place a check next to each number that has **2** in the hundreds place.

287 _____   202 _____

381 _____   422 _____

218 _____   274 _____

902 _____   213 _____

23 _____   200 _____

Piñata Party

Color each number that has **0** in the tens place.

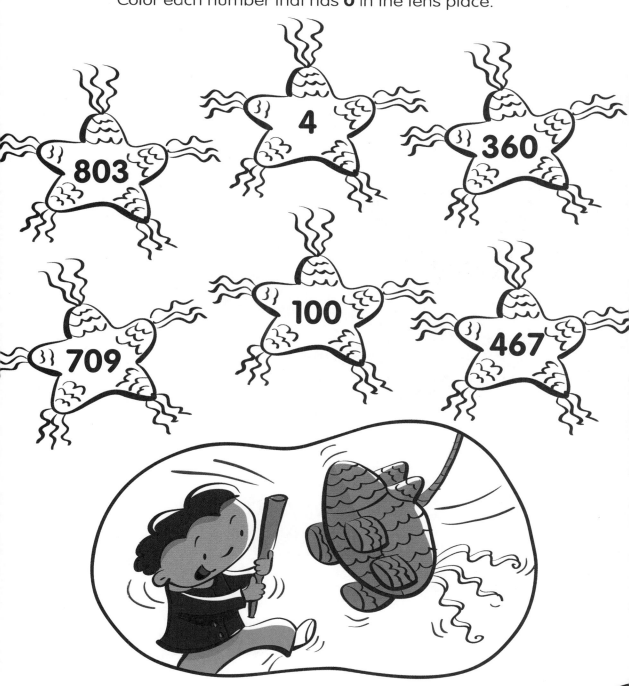

803

4

360

709

100

467

Having a Blast in the Ball Pit

Write how many tens are in each number.

1. **253** _____ tens

2. **719** _____ ten

3. **935** _____ tens

4. **303** _____ tens

5. **123** _____ tens

6. **92** _____ tens

7. **8** _____ tens

8. **293** _____ tens

9. **625** _____ tens

10. **29** _____ tens

Birthday Balloons!

Color the balloons with **8** in the ones place.

712

38

78

800

782

708

621

518

Pool Party

Write the number of hundreds, tens, and ones.

1. **381** = _____ hundreds, _____ tens, _____ one

2. **911** = _____ hundreds, _____ ten, _____ one

3. **842** = _____ hundreds, _____ tens, _____ ones

4. **407** = _____ hundreds, _____ tens, _____ ones

5. **100** = _____ hundred, _____ tens, _____ ones

6. **73** = _____ hundreds, _____ tens, _____ ones

7. **267** = _____ hundreds, _____ tens, _____ ones

8. **306** = _____ hundreds, _____ tens, _____ ones

9. **462** = _____ hundreds, _____ tens, _____ ones

10. **561** = _____ hundreds, _____ tens, _____ one

Bowling Party

Write the number.

1. 7 hundreds + 0 tens + 1 one = _____

2. 2 hundreds + 2 tens + 9 ones = _____

3. 9 hundreds + 1 ten + 3 ones = _____

4. 0 hundreds + 2 tens + 5 ones = _____

5. 4 hundreds + 3 tens + 6 ones = _____

6. 1 hundred + 7 tens + 8 ones = _____

7. 3 hundreds + 6 tens + 2 ones = _____

8. 5 hundreds + 2 tens + 9 ones = _____

9. 8 hundreds + 4 tens + 2 ones = _____

10. 6 hundreds + 5 tens + 0 ones = _____

Popcorn Fun

Circle the numbers in the hundreds place.

Underline the numbers in the tens place.

1. 809

2. 612

3. 593

4. 833

5. 72

6. 844

7. 200

8. 125

9. 86

10. 358

Creative Creatures

Circle the numbers that have **2** in the tens place.

41

29

23

32

722

72

820

247

4

28

Winter Party

Write the number of hundreds, tens, and ones.

1. **582** = _____ hundreds, _____ tens, _____ ones

2. **678** = _____ hundreds, _____ tens, _____ ones

3. **627** = _____ hundreds, _____ tens, _____ ones

4. **50** = _____ hundreds, _____ tens, _____ ones

5. **6** = _____ hundreds, _____ tens, _____ ones

6. **258** = _____ hundreds, _____ tens, _____ ones

7. **195** = _____ hundred, _____ tens, _____ ones

8. **246** = _____ hundreds, _____ tens, _____ ones

9. **981** = _____ hundreds, _____ tens, _____ one

10. **73** = _____ hundreds, _____ tens, _____ ones

Wrap It Up

Place a check to show which place value is circled.

		Hundreds	Tens	Ones
1.	47			
2.	921			
3.	300			
4.	408			
5.	842			
6.	38			

Gotcha!

Color the pieces of candy that have **4** in the hundreds place.

940

475

554

404

487

915

321

448

49

324

Making a Mess

Draw a square around the number in the hundreds place.

Circle the number in the tens place.

Draw a triangle around the number in the ones place.

1. 486
2. 924
3. 48
4. 230
5. 60

6. 570
7. 9
8. 187
9. 364
10. 406

A Quiet Game

Circle the numbers that do not show a number in the hundreds place.

1. 860
2. 58
3. 8
4. 500
5. 67

6. 228
7. 906
8. 56
9. 21
10. 103

Puppet Show

Write the number.

1.   4 hundreds + 0 tens + 9 ones = _____

2.   3 tens + 0 ones = _____

3.   2 hundreds + 1 ten + 0 ones = _____

4.   7 hundreds + 0 tens + 2 ones = _____

5.   5 tens + 2 ones = _____

6.   8 hundreds + 2 tens + 2 ones = _____

7.   6 hundreds + 5 tens + 2 ones = _____

8.   9 hundreds + 2 tens + 3 ones = _____

9.   6 tens + 9 ones = _____

10.   7 hundreds + 2 tens + 3 ones = _____

Make Your Own Sundae

Write how many hundreds are in each number.

1. **482** _____

2. **392** _____

3. **56** _____

4. **90** _____

5. **219** _____

6. **466** _____

7. **294** _____

8. **219** _____

9. **126** _____

10. **502** _____

Party Hats

Color the party hats with **0** in the tens place.

205 405 60

5 700 902

80

A Tea Party

Write the number of hundreds, tens, and ones. Then write the complete number.

1. 2 hundreds + 4 tens + 2 ones

 _200_ + _40_ + _2_ =

 _242_

2. 0 hundreds + 2 tens + 8 ones

 _____ + _____ + _____ =

 _____

3. 7 hundreds + 3 tens + 1 one

 _____ + _____ + _____ =

 _____

4. 6 hundreds + 0 tens + 6 ones

 _____ + _____ + _____ =

 _____

A Thirsty Bunch

Circle the name of the place value that matches
the number that has a square around it.

1.

437

hundreds   tens   ones

2.

3**5**4

hundreds   tens   ones

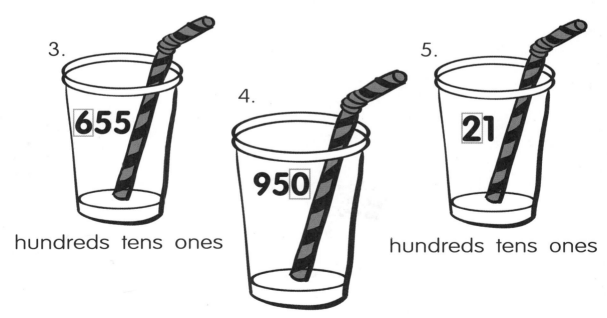

3.

655

hundreds   tens   ones

4.

95**0**

hundreds   tens   ones

5.

21

hundreds   tens   ones

Pig-Out Picnic

Write the number.

1. 3 hundreds + 2 tens + 4 ones = _____

2. 2 hundreds + 1 ten + 9 ones = _____

3. 7 hundreds + 0 tens + 0 ones = _____

4. 6 hundreds + 9 tens + 5 ones = _____

5. 1 hundred + 8 tens + 1 one = _____

6. 4 hundreds + 5 tens + 3 ones = _____

7. 6 hundreds + 3 tens + 8 ones = _____

8. 9 hundreds + 1 ten + 6 ones = _____

9. 2 hundreds + 4 tens + 2 ones = _____

10. 4 hundreds + 3 tens + 4 ones = _____

Bright Idea!

Color the lights that show **6** in the ones place.

Beach Party

Color the beach balls that have **2** in the tens place.

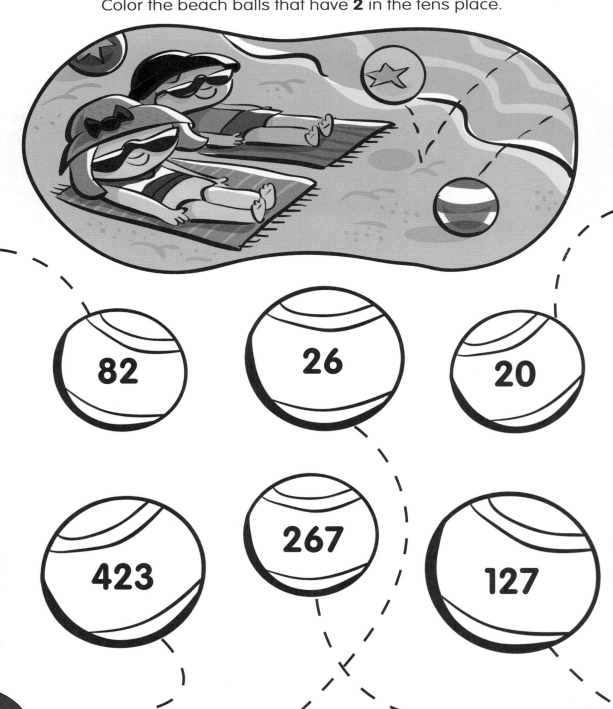

82

26

20

423

267

127

Pumpkin Party

Write the number of hundreds, tens, and ones.
Then write the complete number.

1.

2 hundreds + 0 tens + 6 ones

_____ + _____ + _____ =

_____

2.

1 hundred + 9 tens + 8 ones

_____ + _____ + _____ =

_____

3.

3 hundreds + 2 tens + 3 ones

_____ + _____ + _____ =

_____

4.

4 hundreds + 4 tens + 7 ones

_____ + _____ + _____ =

_____

Baby Party

Write the number of hundreds, tens, and ones.

1. 682 = _____ hundreds, _____ tens, _____ones

2. 820 = _____ hundreds, _____ tens, _____ones

3. 917 = _____ hundreds, _____ ten, _____ones

4. 63 = _____ hundreds, _____ tens, _____ones

5. 577 = _____ hundreds, _____ tens, _____ones

6. 602 = _____ hundreds, _____ tens, _____ones

7. 425 = _____ hundreds, _____ tens, _____ones

8. 396 = _____ hundreds, _____ tens, _____ones

9. 506 = _____ hundreds, _____ tens, _____ones

10. 716 = _____ hundreds, _____ ten, _____ones

Pizza Party

Circle the pieces of pizza that have **9** in the hundreds place.

899

950

909

39

9

994

Puppy Party

Write the number.

1. 5 hundreds + 8 tens + 1 one   = _____

2. 2 hundreds + 2 tens + 2 ones = _____

3. 9 hundreds + 0 tens + 0 ones = _____

4. 0 hundreds + 0 tens + 2 ones = _____

5. 4 hundreds + 2 tens + 9 ones = _____

6. 3 hundreds + 5 tens + 6 ones = _____

7. 7 hundreds + 3 tens + 2 ones = _____

8. 1 hundred + 5 tens + 3 ones = _____

9. 4 hundreds + 6 tens + 2 ones = _____

10. 3 hundreds + 4 tens + 6 ones = _____

Balloons, Balloons, Balloons!

Draw a string on the balloons that have **0** in the ones place.

One More Bow

Write the number of hundreds, tens, and ones. Then write the complete number.

1.   6 hundreds + 8 tens + 4 ones

_____ + _____ + _____ =

_____

2.   3 hundreds + 4 tens + 1 one

_____ + _____ + _____ =

_____

3.   2 hundreds + 5 tens + 0 ones

_____ + _____ + _____ =

_____

4.   4 hundreds + 3 tens + 8 ones

_____ + _____ + _____ =

_____

Balloon Animals

Color the balloon animals that show **3** in the hundreds place.

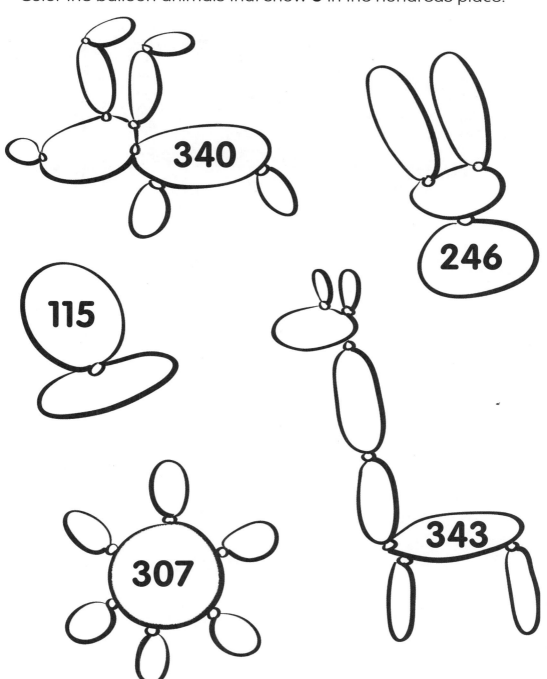

Hide and Seek

Write the number. Pay careful attention to the hundreds, tens, and ones.

1. 8 ones + 2 hundreds + 3 tens = _____

2. 2 tens + 9 ones + 1 hundred = _____

3. 4 hundreds + 0 ones + 5 tens = _____

4. 5 hundreds + 0 tens + 8 ones = _____

5. 7 ones + 1 ten + 2 hundreds = _____

6. 8 tens + 7 ones + 8 hundreds = _____

7. 6 ones + 3 hundreds + 4 tens = _____

8. 7 tens + 2 ones + 3 hundreds = _____

9. 4 hundreds + 5 ones + 6 tens = _____

10. 3 ones + 6 tens + 2 hundreds = _____

Leap Frog Fun

Write the number. Pay careful attention to the hundreds, tens, and ones.

1. 3 tens + 9 ones + 2 hundreds = _____

2. 5 hundreds + 0 tens + 3 ones = _____

3. 6 ones + 7 tens + 1 hundred = _____

4. 4 tens + 0 hundreds + 6 ones = _____

5. 0 tens + 8 ones + 3 hundreds = _____

6. 7 ones + 2 hundreds + 6 tens = _____

7. 3 tens + 2 ones + 7 hundreds = _____

8. 4 ones + 3 hundreds + 2 tens = _____

9. 0 ones + 2 tens + 4 hundreds = _____

10. 6 tens + 7 ones + 3 hundreds = _____

Great Gift!

Check the box that shows the place value that is circled.

		Hundreds	Tens	Ones
1.	4⑧7			
2.	99②			
3.	③5			
4.	②00			
5.	⑤83			
6.	11⑨			

Bows in a Row

Color the bows with **4** in the tens place.

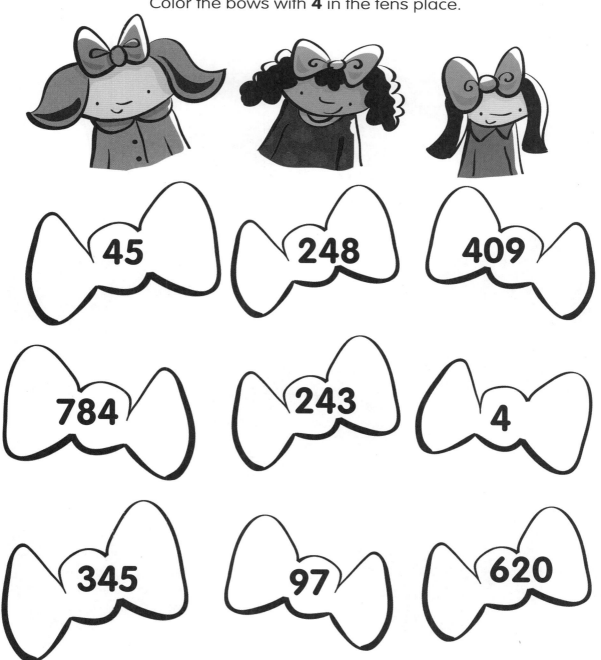

45

248

409

784

243

4

345

97

620

Pajama Party

Circle the number that has a larger tens place.

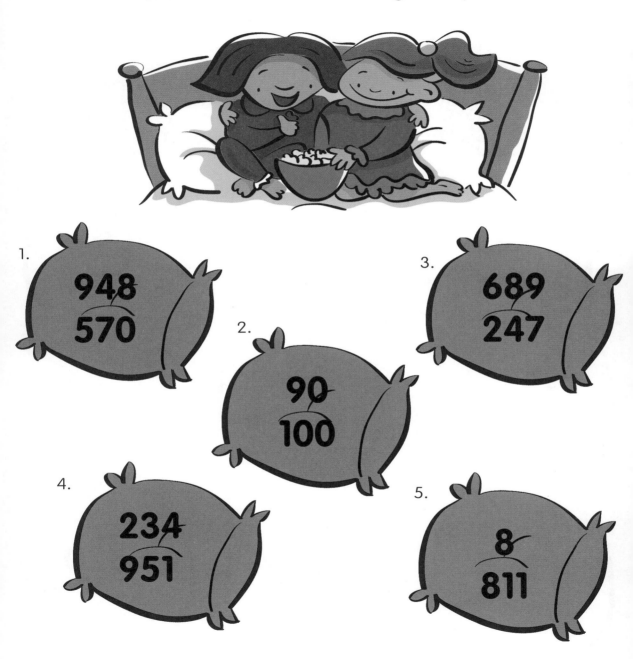

1. 948
   570

2. 90
   100

3. 689
   247

4. 234
   951

5. 8
   811

Party Favors

Circle the number that has a larger ones place.

1. 587
   250

2. 28
   281

3. 630
   782

4. 468
   39

5. 725
   366

Birthday Party

Write the number that has a smaller tens place.

1. 345 890 <u>345</u>

2. 920 832 ___

3. 120 40 ___

4. 567 756 ___

5. 354 12 ___

6. 219 56 ___

7. 406 228 ___

8. 67 170 ___

9. 258 162 ___

10. 119 191 ___

Clean Up Time

Write the number that has a smaller ones place.

1. 50   652   _50_

2. 851   327   ____

3. 25   920   ____

4. 645   728   ____

5. 562   89   ____

6. 221   70   ____

7. 115   106   ____

8. 245   197   ____

9. 310   211   ____

10. 409   510   ____

Musical Chairs

Thousands is the place value after hundreds. 1000 comes after 999.

thousands place   hundreds place   tens place   ones place

There is 1 thousand.

There are 3 hundreds.

There are 7 tens.

There are 5 ones.

Huffing and Puffing

Write the number of thousands, hundreds, tens, and ones.

1. **5,982** = _____ thousands, _____ hundreds, _____ tens, _____ ones

2. **2,855** = _____ thousands, _____ hundreds, _____ tens, _____ ones

3. **1,896** = _____ thousand, _____ hundreds, _____ tens, _____ ones

4. **3,702** = _____ thousands, _____ hundreds, _____ tens, _____ ones

5. **8,008** = _____ thousands, _____ hundreds, _____ tens, _____ ones

6. **3,670** = _____ thousands, _____ hundreds, _____ tens, _____ ones

Wedding Party

Write the number.

1. 3 thousands + 2 hundreds + 9 tens + 8 ones = _____

2. 2 thousands + 1 hundred + 0 tens + 2 ones = _____

3. 8 thousands + 9 hundreds + 2 tens + 4 ones = _____

4. 6 thousands + 5 hundreds + 4 tens + 4 ones = _____

5. 1 thousand + 3 hundreds + 0 tens + 6 ones = _____

6. 2 thousands + 6 hundreds + 9 tens + 0 ones = _____

7. 4 thousands + 3 hundreds + 4 tens + 3 ones = _____

8. 7 thousands + 5 hundreds + 0 tens + 9 ones = _____

Magic Tricks

Write the number that is in the thousands place.

1. **8,920** _____

2. **3,644** _____

3. **2,587** _____

4. **1,010** _____

5. **9,647** _____

6. **4,086** _____

7. **5,000** _____

8. **7,438** _____

9. **8,209** _____

10. **6,321** _____

Time for Treats

Color the ice cream sundaes with the **9** in the thousands place.

9,098

5,890

4,989

1,298

5,486

9,393

9,000

6,524

A Painting Party!

Write how many thousands, hundreds, tens, and ones there are.

		Thousands	Hundreds	Tens	Ones
1.	5,874				
2.	502				
3.	2,588				
4.	632				
5.	30				
6.	8,745				

Potato Sack Race

Write the number.

1. 4 thousands + 2 hundreds + 0 tens + 3 ones = _____

2. 0 thousands + 5 hundreds + 8 tens + 0 ones = _____

3. 3 thousands + 9 hundreds + 5 tens + 8 ones = _____

4. 0 thousands + 0 hundreds + 3 tens + 1 one = _____

5. 5 thousands + 0 hundreds + 4 tens + 2 ones = _____

6. 2 thousands + 1 hundred + 7 tens + 5 ones = _____

Barbeque!

Check the box that shows the place value that is circled.

		Thousands	Hundreds	Tens	Ones
1.	5,820				
2.	632				
3.	7,434				
4.	67				
5.	964				
6.	1,689				

Finger Paints!

Color the hands that have **5** in the hundreds place.

520

7,895

6,250

9,584

5,550

635

5,000

2,500

323

1,500

Bubbles!

Write the number of thousands, hundreds, tens, and ones.

		Thousands	Hundreds	Tens	Ones
1.	784				
2.	505				
3.	4,921				
4.	3,120				
5.	58				
6.	2,689				

Relay Races

Circle the number that has a larger number in the tens place.

1. **7,769**   **6,384**

2. **251**   **7,820**

3. **415**   **4,575**

4. **2,010**   **998**

5. **7,643**   **384**

6. **367**   **3,111**

7. **201**   **99**

8. **1,412**   **2,656**

What a Day!

Circle the number that has a smaller number in the thousands place.

1. **7,589**   **3,697**

2. **4,050**   **6,050**

3. **1,327**   **9,547**

4. **8,522**   **3,987**

5. **5,555**   **8,888**

6. **2,020**   **3,000**

7. **8,129**   **6,092**

8. **6,258**   **3,520**

Answer Key

Page 5
1. 1
2. 2
3. 3

Page 6
1. 43
2. 29
3. 32
4. 11
5. 20
6. 14
7. 49
8. 35
9. 60
10. 55

Page 7
1. 7 tens and 4 ones
2. 5 tens and 2 ones
3. 4 tens and 9 ones
4. 3 tens and 7 ones
5. 1 ten and 0 ones
6. 6 tens and 9 ones
7. 7 tens and 3 ones
8. 5 tens and 5 ones
9. 6 tens and 8 ones
10. 4 tens and 2 ones

Page 8
1. 39
2. 20
3. 71
4. 63
5. 84
6. 15
7. 91

Page 9
The following numbers
should be colored:
14, 34, 4, 24

Page 10
1. 24
2. 3 tens and 0 ones = 30
3. 2 tens and 5 ones = 25
4. 1 ten and 8 ones = 18

Page 11
1. 42
2. 91
3. 10
4. 5
5. 39
6. 36
7. 72
8. 59
9. 22
10. 46

Page 12
1. 137
2. 219
3. 128

Page 13
1. 821
2. 158
3. 571
4. 369
5. 870
6. 300

Page 14
The following numbers
should have a check:
287, 218, 202, 274, 213, 200

Page 15
The following numbers should
be colored: 803, 709, 100

Page 16
1. 5
2. 1
3. 3
4. 0
5. 2
6. 9
7. 0
8. 9
9. 2
10. 2

Page 17
The following numbers should
be colored: 38, 78, 708, 518

Page 18
1. 3 hundreds, 8 tens, 1 one
2. 9 hundreds, 1 ten, 1 one
3. 8 hundreds, 4 tens, 2 ones
4. 4 hundreds, 0 tens, 7 ones
5. 1 hundred, 0 tens, 0 ones
6. 0 hundreds, 7 tens, 3 ones
7. 2 hundreds, 6 tens, 7 ones
8. 3 hundreds, 0 tens, 6 ones
9. 4 hundreds, 6 tens, 2 ones
10. 5 hundreds, 6 tens, 1 one

Page 19
1. 701
2. 229
3. 913
4. 25
5. 436
6. 178
7. 362
8. 529
9. 842
10. 650

Page 20
1. 809
2. 612
3. 593
4. 833
5. 72
6. 844
7. 200
8. 125
9. 86
10. 358

Page 21
The following numbers should
be circled: 29, 23, 722, 820, 28

Page 22
1. 5 hundreds, 8 tens, 2 ones
2. 6 hundreds, 7 tens, 8 ones
3. 6 hundreds, 2 tens, 7 ones
4. 0 hundreds, 5 tens, 0 ones
5. 0 hundreds, 0 tens, 6 ones
6. 2 hundreds, 5 tens, 8 ones
7. 1 hundred, 9 tens, 5 ones
8. 2 hundreds, 4 tens, 6 ones
9. 9 hundreds, 8 tens, 1 one
10. 0 hundreds, 7 tens, 3 ones

Page 23
1. tens
2. ones
3. hundreds
4. ones
5. ones
6. tens

Page 24
The following numbers should
be colored: 487, 475, 404, 448

Page 25
1. 486
2. 924
3. 48
4. 230
5. 60
6. 570
7. 9
8. 187
9. 364
10. 406

Page 26
The following numbers should
be circled: 58, 8, 67, 56, 21

Page 27
1. 409
2. 30
3. 210
4. 702
5. 52
6. 822
7. 652
8. 923
9. 69
10. 723

Page 28
1. 4
2. 3
3. 0
4. 0
5. 2
6. 4
7. 2
8. 2
9. 1
10. 5

Page 29
The following numbers
should be colored:
205, 405, 700, 902

Page 30
2. 0 + 20 + 8 = 28
3. 700 + 30 + 1 = 731
4. 600 + 0 + 6 = 606

Page 31
1. hundreds
2. tens
3. hundreds
4. ones
5. tens

Page 32
1. 324
2. 219
3. 700
4. 695
5. 181
6. 453
7. 638
8. 916
9. 242
10. 434

Page 33
The following numbers
should be colored:
46, 896, 6, 86

Page 34
The following numbers
should be colored:
26, 20, 423, 127

Page 35
1. 200 + 0 + 6 = 206
2. 100 + 90 + 8 = 198
3. 300 + 20 + 3 = 323
4. 400 + 40 + 7 = 447

Page 36
1. 6 hundreds, 8 tens, 2 ones
2. 8 hundreds, 2 tens, 0 ones
3. 9 hundreds, 1 ten, 7 ones
4. 0 hundreds, 6 tens, 3 ones
5. 5 hundreds, 7 tens, 7 ones
6. 6 hundreds, 0 tens, 2 ones
7. 4 hundreds, 2 tens, 5 ones
8. 3 hundreds, 9 tens, 6 ones
9. 5 hundreds, 0 tens, 6 ones
10. 7 hundreds, 1 ten, 6 ones

Page 37
The following numbers
should be circled:
950, 909, 994

Page 38
1. 581   6. 356
2. 222   7. 732
3. 900   8. 153
4. 2   9. 462
5. 429   10. 346

Page 39
The following balloons
should have a string:
10, 300, 90, 30

Page 40
1. 600 + 80 + 4 = 684
2. 300 + 40 + 1 = 341
3. 200 + 50 + 0 = 250
4. 400 + 30 + 8 = 438

Page 41
The following numbers
should be colored:
340, 343, 307

Page 42
1. 238   6. 887
2. 129   7. 346
3. 450   8. 372
4. 508   9. 465
5. 217   10. 263

Page 43
1. 239   6. 267
2. 503   7. 732
3. 176   8. 324
4. 46   9. 420
5. 308   10. 367

Page 44
1. tens   4. hundreds
2. ones   5. hundreds
3. tens   6. ones

Page 45
The following numbers
should be colored:
45, 248, 243, 345

Page 46
The following numbers
should be circled:
1. 570 2. 90 3. 689
4. 951 5. 811

Page 47
The following numbers
should be circled:
1. 587 2. 28 3. 782
4. 39 5. 366

Page 48
2. 920   6. 219
3. 120   7. 406
4. 756   8. 67
5. 12   9. 258
            10. 119

Page 49
2. 851   6. 70
3. 920   7. 115
4. 645   8. 245
5. 562   9. 310
            10. 510

Page 51
1. 5 thousands, 9 hundreds,
   8 tens, 2 ones
2. 2 thousands, 8 hundreds,
   5 tens, 5 ones
3. 1 thousand, 8 hundreds,
   9 tens, 6 ones
4. 3 thousands, 7 hundreds,
   0 tens, 2 ones
5. 8 thousands, 0 hundreds,
   0 tens, 8 ones
6. 3 thousands, 6 hundreds,
   7 tens, 0 ones

Page 52
1. 3,298   5. 1,306
2. 2,102   6. 2,690
3. 8,924   7. 4,343
4. 6,544   8. 7,509

Page 53
1. 8   6. 4
2. 3   7. 5
3. 2   8. 7
4. 1   9. 8
5. 9   10. 6

Page 54
The following numbers should
be colored: 9,098; 9,393; 9,000

Page 55
1. 5 thousands, 8 hundreds,
   7 tens, 4 ones
2. 0 thousands, 5 hundreds,
   0 tens, 2 ones
3. 2 thousands, 5 hundreds,
   8 tens, 8 ones
4. 0 thousands, 6 hundreds,
   3 tens, 2 ones
5. 0 thousands, 0 hundreds,
   3 tens, 0 ones
6. 8 thousands, 7 hundreds,
   4 tens, 5 ones

Page 56
1. 4,203   4. 31
2. 580   5. 5,042
3. 3,958   6. 2,175

Page 57
1. hundreds   4. ones
2. ones   5. tens
3. thousands   6. thousands

Page 58
The following numbers
should be colored: 520;
9,584; 5,550; 2,500; 1,500

Page 59
1. 0 thousands, 7 hundreds,
   8 tens, 4 ones
2. 0 thousands, 5 hundreds,
   0 tens, 5 ones
3. 4 thousands, 9 hundreds,
   2 tens, 1 one
4. 3 thousands, 1 hundred,
   2 tens, 0 ones
5. 0 thousands, 0 hundreds,
   5 tens, 8 ones
6. 2 thousands, 6 hundreds,
   8 tens, 9 ones

Page 60
These numbers
should be circled:
1. 6,384   5. 384
2. 251   6. 367
3. 4,575   7. 99
4. 998   8. 2,656

Page 61
These numbers
should be circled:
1. 3,697   5. 5,555
2. 4,050   6. 2,020
3. 1,327   7. 6,092
4. 3987   8. 3,520